W9-CLF-501

Comparing Past and Present

Going to the Doctor

Rebecca Rissman

Heinemann
LIBRARY

Chicago, Illinois

SOUTH HUNTINGTON
PUBLIC LIBRARY
145 PIDGEON HILL RD
HUNT. STA., NY 11746

© 2014 Heinemann Library
an imprint of Capstone Global Library, LLC
Chicago, Illinois

To contact Capstone Global Library please phone 800-747-4992, or visit our website www.capstonepub.com

All rights reserved. No part of this publication may be reproduced or transmitted in any form or by any means, electronic or mechanical, including photocopying, recording, taping, or any information storage and retrieval system, without permission in writing from the publisher.

Edited by Rebecca Rissman, Daniel Nunn, and
   Catherine Veitch
Designed by Philippa Jenkins
Picture research by Elizabeth Alexander
Production by Helen McCreath
Originated by Capstone Global Library Ltd
Printed and bound in China

17 16 15 14 13
10 9 8 7 6 5 4 3 2 1

Library of Congress Cataloging-in-Publication Data
Rissman, Rebecca.
  Going to the doctor / Rebecca Rissman.
     pages cm.—(Comparing past and present)
  Includes bibliographical references and index.
  ISBN 978-1-4329-8992-7 (hb)—ISBN 978-1-4329-9026-8 (pb)
1. Medical care—History—Juvenile literature. 2. Physicians—Juvenile literature. 3. Health—Juvenile literature. I. Title.
  R130.5.R57 2014
  610—dc23   2013012544

Acknowledgments
We would like to thank the following for permission to reproduce photographs: Alamy pp. 5 (© YAY Media AS), 7 (© Tetra Images), 8 (© Old Visuals), 9 (© Blend Images), 11 (© jozef mikietyn), 23 (© jozef mikietyn); Corbis pp. 6 (© Alinari Archives), 16 (© H Bedford Lemere/English Heritage), 18 (© Bettmann), 23 (© H Bedford Lemere/English Heritage); Getty Images pp. 4 (A. R. Coster/Topical Press Agency/Hulton Archive), 10 (Fox Photos/Hulton Archive), 12 (Vintage Images), 17 (Halfdark/the Agency Collection), 23 (Halfdark/the Agency Collection); Mary Evans p. 14 (Sueddeutsche Zeitung Photo); Shutterstock pp. 13 (© CandyBox Images), 15 (© mangostock), 19 (© wavebreakmedia), 21 (© Monkey Business Images), 23 (© wavebreakmedia); SuperStock pp. 20 (ClassicStock.com), 22.

Front cover photographs of a sick child receiving a bunch of daffodils reproduced with permission of Getty Images (Fox Photos/Hulton Archive), and a doctor checking a child patient reproduced with permission of Getty Images (SelectStock/the Agency Collection). Back cover photograph of a doctor talking to a patient reproduced with permission of Superstock.

We would like to thank Nancy Harris and Diana Bentley for their invaluable help in the preparation of this book.

Every effort has been made to contact copyright holders of material reproduced in this book. Any omissions will be rectified in subsequent printings if notice is given to the publisher.

Contents

Comparing the Past and Present

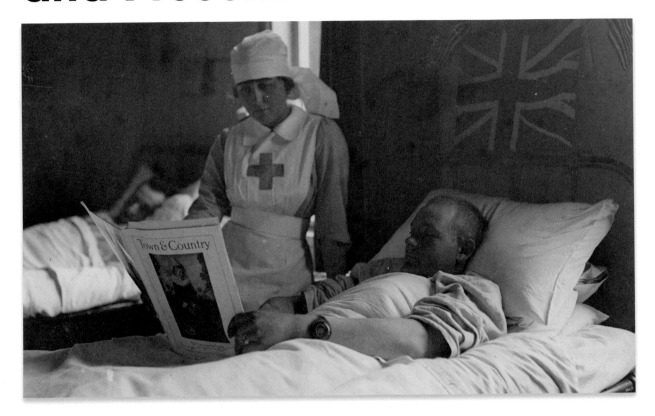

Things in the past have already happened.

Things in the present are happening now.

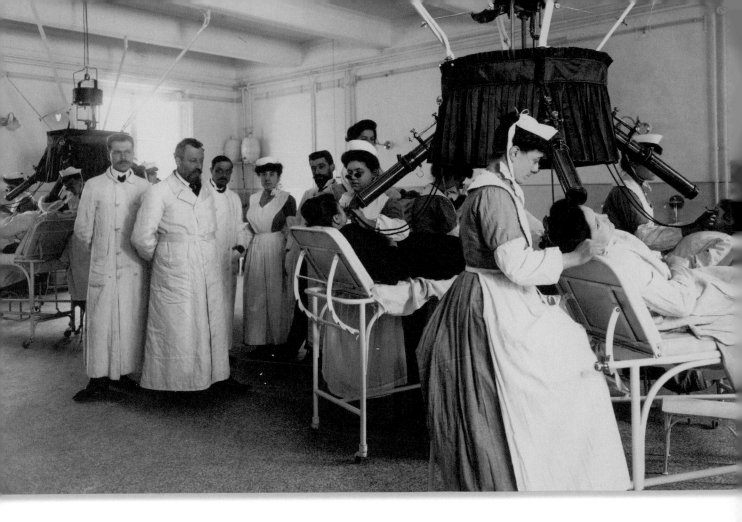

Going to the doctor has changed over time.

The way people go to the doctor today is very different from the past.

Seeing the Doctor

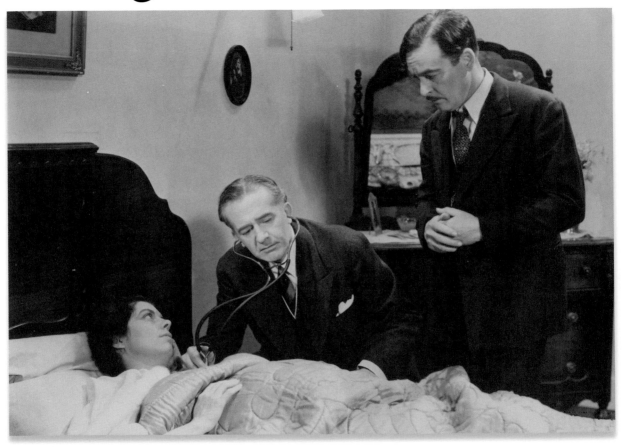

In the past, some doctors visited the homes of sick people.

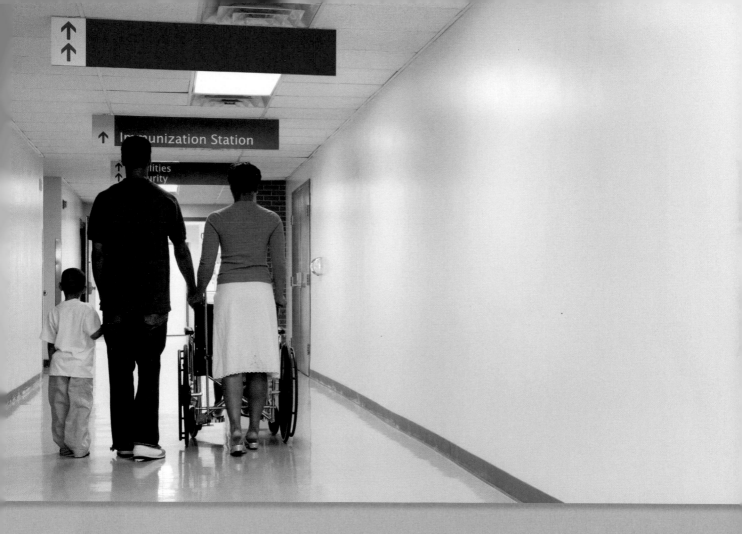

Today, most people see a doctor
at a clinic or hospital.

Getting to the Doctor

In the past, some people went a long way to see the doctor.

Today, most people live close to a clinic or hospital.

In the past, some sick people went to the hospital in ambulance carts.

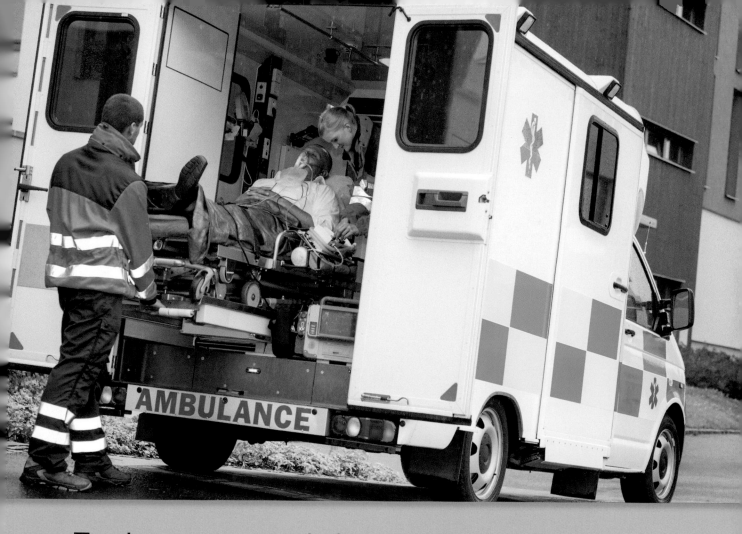

Today, some sick people get to
a hospital in an ambulance.

Medicine

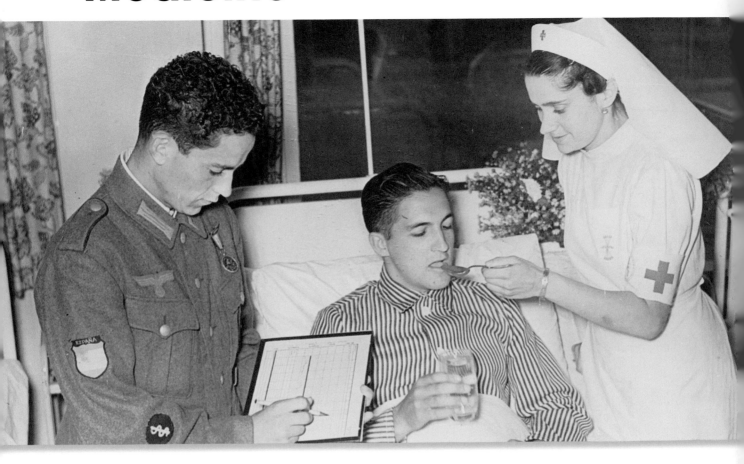

In the past, doctors had few medicines to help sick people.

Today, there are many medicines
to help people get better.

Hospitals

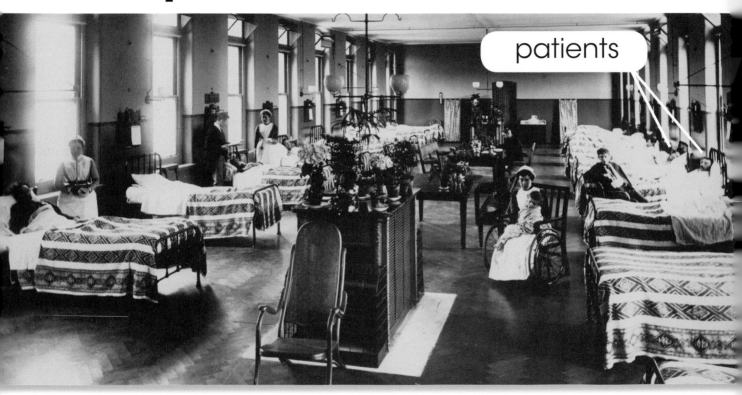

patients

In the past, hospitals were made up of large rooms. Many patients stayed in the same room.

Today, hospitals are made up of many small rooms. Fewer patients stay in the same room.

Doctors and Nurses

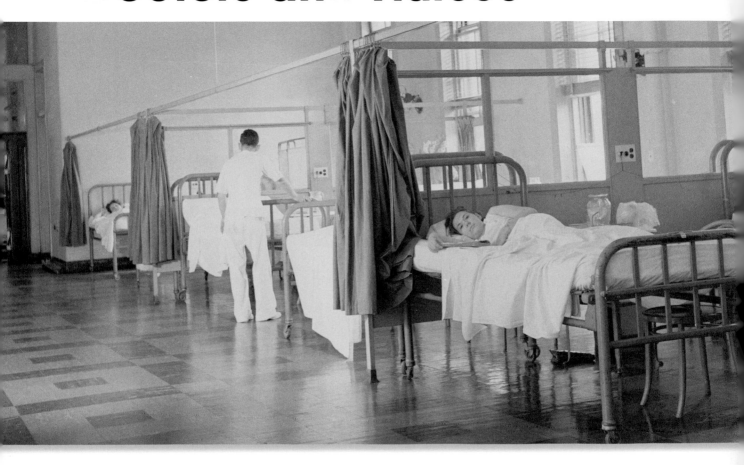

In the past, hospitals had fewer doctors.

Today, hospitals have many doctors.

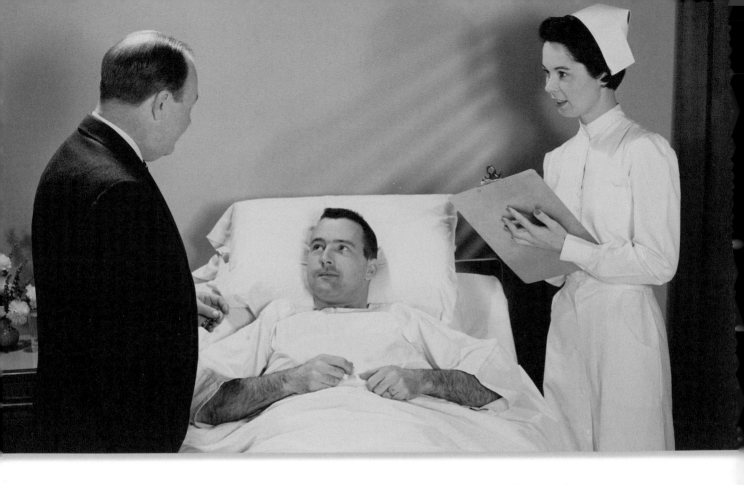

In the past, nurses and doctors helped patients at the hospital.

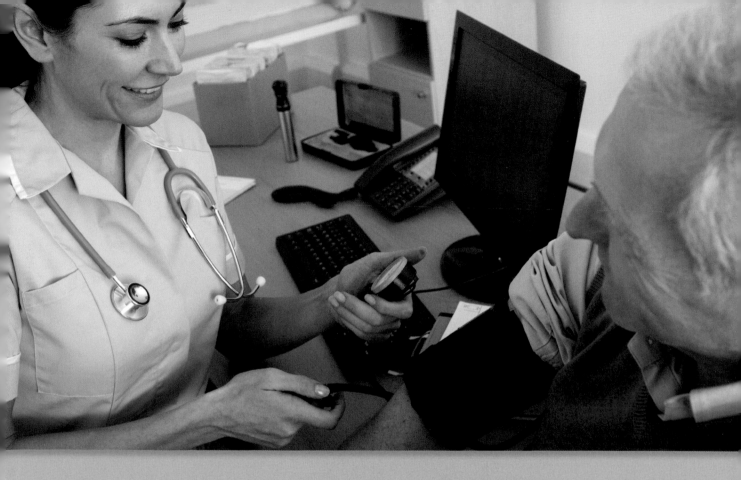

Today, nurses and doctors also
help patients at the hospital.

Then and Now

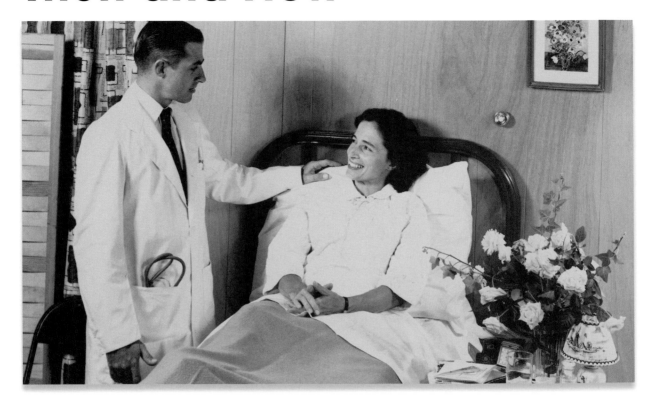

In the past, doctors did their best to help sick patients. Today, doctors still do their best to help sick patients.

Picture Glossary

clinic place where doctors see their patients

hospital place where doctors and nurses work to care for patients

nurse person who works in a hospital helping to care for patients

patient person visiting a doctor for medicine or medical care

Index

Note to Parents and Teachers

Before reading

Teach children about the difference between the past and present. Explain to children that things that have already happened are in the past. To help them understand this concept, ask children to tell you about what they ate for breakfast. Then, explain to them that their breakfast happened in the past. Tell children that your conversation is happening in the present.

After reading

- Explain to children that the way people visit the doctor has changed over time. Ask children to describe their last visit to a doctor. Encourage them to think about driving to the doctor's office, whether they saw a nurse, and what the office looked like.

- Ask children to look at the images on pages 12–13. Can they think of any ways the images are different? Can they think of why it might be helpful to get to the hospital quickly?

- Show children the image on page 15. Explain that today, many medicines exist to help people heal from different sicknesses. Ask children how life in the past might have been more difficult with fewer medicines.

AUG 2 4 2014 19(4)

2199

(7(3)